Increaible Adventures

Based on an original text by Simon Adams
Reading consultants: Christopher Collier and Alan Howe,
Bath Spa University, UK

First published by Parragon in 2009
Parragon
Queen Street House
4 Queen Street
Bath BA1 1HE, UK

ISBN 978-1-4075-8859-9

Printed in China

Incredible Adventures

LIVE. LEARN. DISCOVER.

Bath New York Singapore Hong Kong Cologne Delhi Melbourne

Parents' notes

This book is part of a series of nonfiction books designed to appeal to children learning to read.

Each book has been developed with the help of educational experts.

At the end of each book is a quiz to help your child remember the information and the meanings of some of the words and sentences. There is also a glossary of difficult words relating to the subject matter in the book, and an index.

Contents

The Vikings

The Vikings, or Norsemen, were important early explorers. They came from Denmark, Norway, and Sweden. Between 800 and 1400, they set sail in search of new lands to live in.

Crossing the oceans in Viking boats was very dangerous.

The Vikings
found their way
across the oceans
using only the sun
and stars.

The Vikings were the first **Europeans** to visit North America. Leif Eriksson visited North America in about 1000.

The Vikings made new homes in Ireland, Scotland, the Faeroe Islands, Iceland, Greenland, and Canada. The villages looked like this.

The Polos

In the 1200s, Niccolo, Maffeo, and Marco Polo traveled from Italy to China. At that time, travel to other lands was difficult and often dangerous.

Venice

ITALY

Black Sea

Constantinople (Istanbul)

TURKEY

Baku

Caspian Sea

Bo

Mosul

Sava PERSIA

Mediterranean Sea

Acre Baghdad

Jerusalem

Kerman

AFRICA

Hormuz

ARABIA

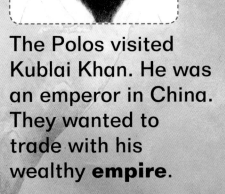

This picture is of Marco Polo. He was Niccolo's son. He was just 17 years old when he left Italy.

The Polos visited Kublai Khan. He was an emperor in China. They wanted to trade with his wealthy **empire**.

On their way to China, the Polos had to cross the Gobi Desert. It was very dangerous.

Gobi Desert   MONGOLIA

Kashgar ••••••••••••••••••••••• Shang-du

Khotan   Lop   Khanbaliq (Beijing)

Marco Polo lived in China for 20 years. He worked for Kublai Khan and traveled in China and other parts of Asia. Eventually, he returned to Italy.

Kinsay (Hangzhou)

CHINA

Zaiton (Amoy)

INDIA

Bay of Bengal

Ocean

South China Sea

◄--- The Polos' route to Khanbaliq (1271–75)

◄--- Marco Polo's travels while working for Kublai Khan

──── The Polos' route home to Venice (1292–95)

SUMATRA   BORNEO

JAVA

9

Portuguese explorers

Between 1400 and 1500, Portuguese explorers sailed from Europe to India and China. They sailed around Africa and across the Indian Ocean.

This picture shows a **map** of India that Portuguese explorers made.

The Portuguese invented a new kind of ship called a caravel. It was good at surviving storms.

In 1488, Bartholomeu Dias and his crew were the first men to sail around the southern tip of Africa.

In 1497–99, Vasco da Gama and his crew were the first men to sail from Europe to India and back again. Only one-fourth of the crew survived the journey.

Discovering the Americas

In 1492, Christopher Columbus discovered the Americas by accident. He was actually trying to sail to Asia!

Columbus set sail from Palos, Spain, with three ships. There was the *Niña* (left), the *Santa Maria* (center), and the *Pinta* (right).

European explorers discovered new fruit and vegetables in the Americas, such as pineapples, potatoes, and corn.

Columbus landed in the West Indies and discovered Cuba and Haiti. But he believed he had landed in India!

There were already people living in the Americas when Columbus landed. He met a tribe called the Arawaks. The people already living in the Americas were often treated very cruelly by European explorers.

Sailing around the world

In 1522, Ferdinand Magellan's crew were the first people to sail around the world.

corn

Magellan did not mean to sail around the world. He was trying to sail to Asia to buy spices, such as the ones in this picture.

EUROPE

Spain

AFRICA

Atlantic Ocean

SOUTH AMERICA

Pacific Ocean

This map shows Magellan's route around the world. He set off with five Spanish ships.

Strait of Magellan

Magellan died on the voyage. He died in a battle in the Philippines.

Magellan's crew went on without him. The voyage took them three years. Only 17 out of 250 men survived. The *Victoria* was the only ship to ake it home.

ASIA

dian Ocean

Ma

Phi

d

Pacific Ocean

Spice Islands

Southern Ocean

Discovering Australia and New Zealand

Europeans discovered Australia and New Zealand in the 1600s and 1700s. But other explorers had discovered these lands long before.

About 40,000 years ago, the **Aborigines** walked from Asia to Australia. They walked across land that today is underneath the sea.

In about the year 1000, **Polynesian** explorers discovered New Zealand. They sailed in boats like these.

boat

stars

Leif Eriksson

Gobi Desert

Kublai Khan

Christopher Columbus

pineapples

potatoes

Ferdinand Magellan

Aborigine

spices

kangaroo

Captain James Cook

William Clark

husky dog

Robert Peary

outback

camels

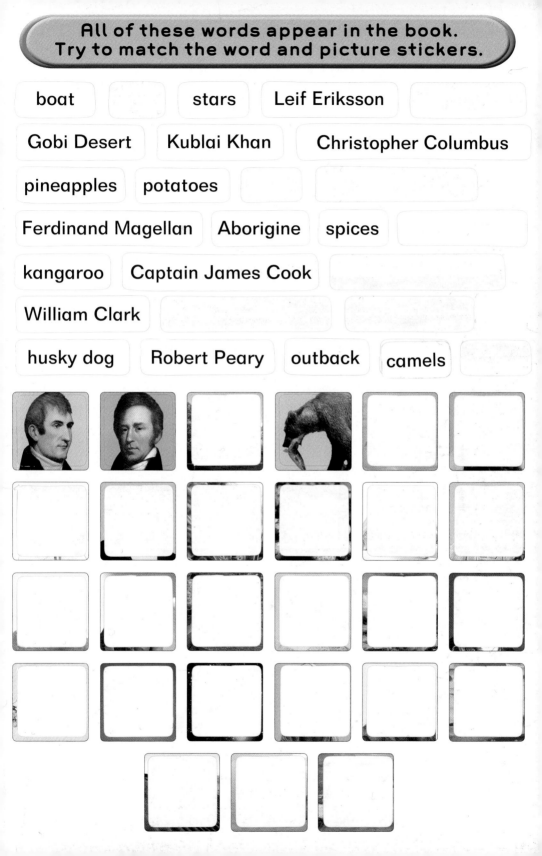

Between 1642 and 1644, the Dutch explorer Abel Tasman sailed around Australia and New Zealand.

On April 29, 1770, the Englishman Captain James Cook landed at Botany Bay in Australia. Cook's crew were the first Europeans to see kangaroos, such as this one.

Lewis and Clark

In 1803, President Thomas Jefferson bought a big piece of land in North America from the French. He asked Meriwether Lewis and William Clark to explore it. He asked them to find a route from the east to the west coast of North America.

Lewis and Clark's **expedition** had to cross the Rocky Mountains.

Lewis and Clark met while they were in the army. They were a very good team.

Lewis and Clark spent one winter with a friendly **Native American** tribe called the Mandan

The expedition reached the Pacific coast in November 1805. It had taken two years to cross the American **continent**.

Grizzly bears attacked the expedition in the Rocky Mountains. One bear chased six men into a river.

Crossing Australia

In 1860, the South Australian **government** offered a prize. The prize would be given to the first person to travel across the Australian continent from the south coast to the north coast.

The center of Australia is hard to travel through because it is so hot and dry. It is called sun utback.

DiscoveryFact™

Australian travelers used camels to help them travel through the outback.

John McDouall Stuart wanted to win the prize. He made three attempts to cross Australia in two years!

In October 1861, McDouall Stuart reached the north coast of Australia. The continent had been crossed at last.

David Livingstone

David Livingstone was one of the greatest European explorers of Africa.

Livingstone lived in Africa for over 30 years. He made four great journeys. They are shown on this map. He died during the final journey.

Livingstone came from a poor family in Scotland. He was a doctor and a **missionary** as well as an explorer.

Livingstone discovered new lakes. He made the first maps of many important rivers. This is Lake Bangweulu.

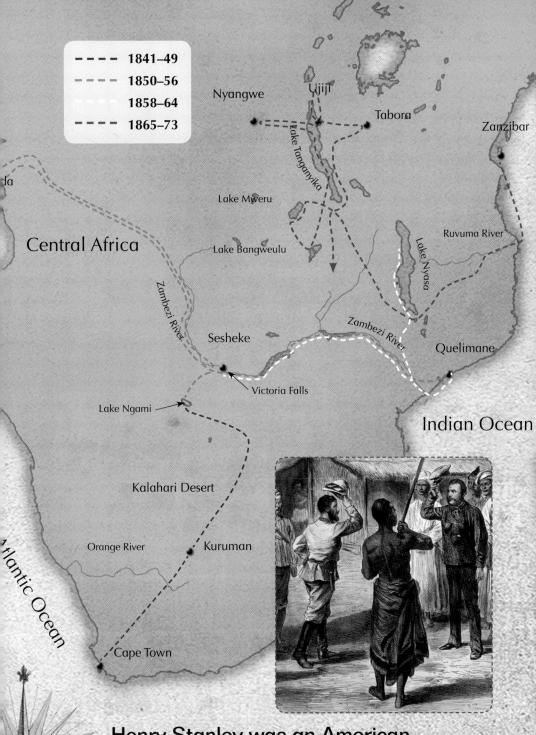

– – –	1841–49
– – –	1850–56
– – –	1858–64
– – –	1865–73

Nyangwe

Ujiji

Tabora

Zanzibar

Lake Tanganyika

Lake Mweru

Ruvuma River

Central Africa

Lake Bangweulu

Lake Nyasa

da

Zambezi River

Sesheke

Zambezi River

Quelimane

Victoria Falls

Lake Ngami

Indian Ocean

Kalahari Desert

Orange River

Kuruman

Atlantic Ocean

Cape Town

Henry Stanley was an American **journalist**. In 1871, he traveled over 700 miles to find and talk to Livingstone.

Race to the Poles

The **North Pole** is in the Arctic. The **South Pole** is in the Antarctic. In both places, it is very cold and dangerous.

Arctic and Antarctic explorers used husky dogs to pull sleds. Husky dogs have thick fur. They can survive very cold weather.

Marco Polo

In 1909, American Robert Peary's team were probably the first people to reach the North Pole.

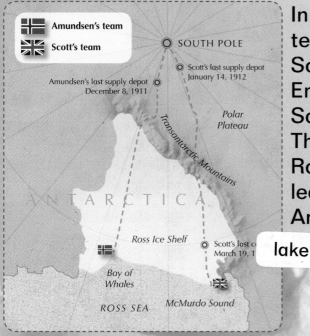

Amundsen's team
Scott's team

SOUTH POLE

Scott's last supply depot
January 14, 1912

Amundsen's last supply depot
December 8, 1911

Polar
Plateau

Transantarctic Mountains

ANTARCTICA

Ross Ice Shelf

Scott's last c...
March 19, 1...

lake

Bay of
Whales

McMurdo Sound

ROSS SEA

In 1911, two teams raced to the South Pole. The Englishman Robert Scott led one team. The Norwegian Roald Amundsen led the other team. Amundsen won ____ race.

Scott and his team all died on the journey back. They were not well enough prepared for the cold weather.

Rocky Mountains

Quiz

Now try this quiz!

All the answers can be found in this book.

Who were the first Europeans to visit North America?

(a) The Spanish
(b) The English
(c) The Vikings

Where did the Polo family travel to?

(a) America
(b) Australia
(c) China

Where was Columbus trying to sail to?

(a) Africa
(b) America
(c) Asia

What mountains did Lewis and Clark have to cross?

(a) The Himalayan Mountains
(b) The Rocky Mountains
(c) The Andes Mountains

What is the center of Australia called?

(a) The outback
(b) The Australian Desert
(c) The Great Space

Who was the first person to reach the South Pole?

(a) Robert Scott
(b) Roald Amundsen
(c) Robert Peary

Glossary

Aborigine   The people who lived in Australia before Europeans arrived.

Continent   A big mass of land. Earth has seven continents. They are Europe, North America, South America, Asia, Oceania, Africa, and Antarctica.

Empire   A very large area of the world ruled by one government. The person who rules an empire is called an emperor or an empress.

European   Someone who comes from the continent of Europe.

Expedition   A difficult journey.

Government   The group of people who run a country.

Journalist   Someone who writes for a newspaper or magazine.

Map   A drawing of an area of the
                   earth. People use maps to help
                   them figure out which way to go.

Missionary   A person who travels to another
                   country to convert the local people
                   to his or her religion.

Native   The people who lived in the
American   Americas before Europeans
                   arrived.

North Pole   The North Pole is the very top
                   of the earth.

Polynesian   The people who live on the
                   islands in the Pacific Ocean.

South Pole   The South Pole is the very bottom
                   of the earth.

Index

Acknowledgments

t=top, c=center, b=bottom, r=right, l=left

Artwork supplied by Martin McKenna, Michael Welply, and Mike White, and through Linden Artists by Adam Hook, Francis Phillips, and Clive Spong

Photo credits

Front cover: Getty Images/VisionsofAmerica/Joe Sohm

3 istockphoto/Denise Kappa, 5 tl Krause, Johansen/Archivo Iconografico, SA/Corbis, 5 cl Bettmann/Corbis, 5 b Stapleton Collection/Corbis, 7 tl istockphoto/Manfred Konrad, 7tr istockphoto/ Denise Kappa, 7 b Dylan Kereluk/creativecommons.org, 8 br Hulton-Deutsch Collection/Corbis, 9 tr istockphoto/ Xiaoping Liang, 10-11 John Van Hasselt/CORBIS SYGMA, 11 tl The Art Archive/Corbis, 11 tr Krause, Johansen/Archivo Iconografico, SA/Corbis, 13 tr Bettmann/ Corbis, 13 tl Dreamstime.com/Tradkelly, 14 tl Frans Lemmens/zefa/ Corbis, 16-17 istockphoto/Michael Willis, 16 bl Penny Tweedie/Corbis, 17 br National Archive of Canada, 18-19 dreamstime.com/Martin Brown, 18 br Independence National Historical Park, 19 tl Smithsonian American Art Museum, 19 tr istockphoto/Nicholas Roemmelt, 19 br dreamstime.com/Michael Thompson, 20-21 istockphoto/Robb Cox, 20b dreamstime.com/Antonela Magzan, 21 tr John McDouall Stuart Society, 22 bl istockphoto.com/Hulton Archive, 23 br Bettmann/ Corbis, 24-25 dreamtime.com/Bernard Breton, 24 cl U.S. Library of Congress, 25 cr Bettmann/Corbis